SUNNY
WEDNESDAY

SUNNY WEDNESDAY

NOELLE KOCOT

WAVE BOOKS

SEATTLE NEW YORK

Published by Wave Books
www.wavepoetry.com

Wave Books titles are distributed to the trade by
Consortium Book Sales and Distribution
Phone: 800-283-3572 / SAN 631-760X

This title is available in limited edition hardcover
directly from the publisher

Library of Congress Cataloging-in-Publication Data:

Kocot, Noelle.
 Sunny Wednesday / Noelle Kocot. — 1st ed.
    p. cm.
 ISBN 978-1-933517-39-1 (pbk. : alk. paper)
 I. Title.
 PS3611.O36S86 2009
 811'.6—dc22

Grateful acknowledgment is made to the following publications where some of these poems
first appeared: *Absent, The Asthmatic, Conduit, Court Green, Jacket, The Laurel Review, LIT,
LUNGFULL!, New American Writing, Parthenon West Review, Pilot, Seconds: A Visual Treasury of
Verse, Small Press Traffic, Suspect Thoughts, Tin House, Tuesday: An Art Project*

Designed and composed by Stewart A. Williams
Printed in the United States of America

9 8 7 6 5 4 3 2 1

FIRST EDITION

Wave Books 017

Contents

THIS BOOK IS DEDICATED TO PAUL VLACHOS
AND LIZZETTE POTTHOFF

Beyond Recognition

Everyone who came to see the corpse
Of the holy man was struck by his or her own decay.
Even the most skeptical of the throng,
The ones who would no doubt be deemed insane
Among the blue world of souls,
Had to admit there was no odor
Souring the crowded room
Beyond the whiffs of muddled breath
That escaped their every gasp.
And yet they yearned for something else,
Especially the kind and simple ones:
This whirling dance of awe would never be
Enough to discern those signs
With fiery arrows pointing this way, no that way.
These longed to know the difference
Between the unredeemable torque of the lost ones'
Vagaries spiraling past the very edge
Of all their days, and the straight
Path's satellite roving between here and There.
They longed for a meaning more distinct
As they tried and tried in vain
To master the arc of their spiritual trapeze.
And it was these the holy man would have loved,
Would have strummed his fingers across
Their souls as if they were silver-stringed tanburs,
Would have drawn them to him like a strong magnet
Across a wire-like bridge.
And when the fire was finally stoked
With the hallowed body,
Still completely fresh after over a week
Of respects, envy, and tears,
The ones who looked into it first
Saw that man's face smiling beyond
Its melting eye sockets, leaking the secret

They ardently wanted to hear
Even as they could feel each of their own cells
Collapsing daily now, a secret that this man,
Henceforth the professor of all their days and ways,
Who would blow the scales from their eyes
Like a strong wind, the secret he would whisper
To them in the sorrowful music of fallen leaves
Sheeting the sidewalks like mirrors
Under their weary feet,
And it had to do with asking,
The secret had to do with simply asking.

Winter Dedication

An intense gaze both unites
And isolates those exchanging it.
Likewise, the embryonic life
That surrounds us in the spring
Detaches itself from our knife-
Like vision as easily as a wayward kite
From its frayed string.
But this morning, as the day spilled
Starkly through the window,
I didn't look at you at all
And rose more effortlessly
Than your slight sigh would admit.
And although you have the will
Of wild birds, you slept on
In the bluing snow's elusive light
As the stars went out one by one.

To You, the Only

We breathe out our measures
Through a wax paper blizzard.
Two beasts following the creases in the earth's muscle,
A Xanadu of icicles dripping into our hearth of years.

And when I am lost,
Your scent wafts toward me
Like the notes of a vibraphone
And I shake off the muck of existence,

An elegiac ox leaping feet first
Through an opening in a honeycomb
To remind you that before all else we are animals full of music
Tethered to the contradictions of this world.

Here, Kitty Kitty

Even the ticklish crook
Of an arm bothers me more today
Than the incessant honking
Of newborn geese imprinted

With the human. White hyphens
Of the conscious dash signals
Upon the waves of the unconscious,
And I'll tell you frankly,

Right now I don't care what any of it means.
Better to suck my energy from a tea bag,
Rise up out of the placenta
Of an electric blanket,

Brush the shards from my shoulders
And merely observe how they tear
Apart the cozy air.
Better to keep on walking,

Mumbling a song of soft
Sad clauses like someone in love,
Leaving a trail of rubies
Like bullet holes across the faded

Forehead of the snow.
Then, to dive off a precipice,
Purveying the struggles reflected
In the bodies of the intoxicated

And amused tugging at the edges
Of a continent as at a mother's shredded hem.
Better that the glyphs of my imagining
See them off in the crammed

Rockets of my sense while the sky
Pours down a cider of my own devising
Over an arc of trees.
Maybe then the inside story

Will unfold, as primitive as the rain,
As you felt sure it would all along
If you could only just cajole it

So that finally it would leap up purring
Into your open hands.

Light in the Hall

You hadn't slept all night.
Tender as a serenade of angels dancing upon plaster casts,
You waited for the world's greeting
Archived in a viscous void.

You assumed the prayerful posture of a shade
Ready for ascension through chapped lips,
The blinding brightness of the golden section
Wedged into a duel of music.

The pangs of a faraway oblivion
Stuffed in the gullet of each moment
As you watched the stoned evening go as it goes.
And when waves dived finally into the eternal

Waxing and waning of a single breeze,
You'll find the zeros of your soul are no less blue
When they circle the wooden eyes of sleep.
And if the aging mothers fixed you an amulet of whitest sky,

Would your body launch a scream of good-byes
To the legacy of desires that unhinge themselves
Over cribs of shattered nebulae?
The air is wrung into fine lines.

It is like being caught in a shining place
That nails a message to the distances
Singing of a future as light as cork
With nothing to our names but what we've given away.

But if you desired the semiprecious stones of lies,
What would remain in those haggard sockets full of rainwater
When the blizzard of your thoughts muffles
The morning of your gray amends?

What question wakes in forgotten depths
As occult truths arrange themselves in saucers,
Each poured with the faith in a miracle that never falters,
That buoys you to the surface of colors and of forms?

What legend inscribed on insect husks will be exacted
From ancestral thirsts in this tin exquisite whine of hours
While memories gone forever
Tumble through the turnstiles of the dark?

For now, everything is in its natural place.
Lay yourself down, a heavy sleeping sphinx,
In wings of inverted butterflies pressed beneath your lids

While the yellow slippers of your nightmares
Sink through linoleum into the grave.

Rite

Nothing remains of your abrupt presence
Of seeing and suffering, a geography of smoke
Through which the dense air presses,
Lit by the electricity of your human shape

Threading the streets of non-being.
But I have seen your face,
Stained with the obsequies that bleed their halos
Into gutters, while the peristalses of sewers

Offered up their arrowy grime.
I asked, Who would believe any of it,
The cadence of the shrouded pyramidal forms
And the faraway calls of the ones who waited?

I want to lie here and forget my life
With its processions of twilight.
I want to forget that I live gripping the momentum
Of another time vying for the wreath of my bones

And in the pinch of the eventual lapse back
Into the clenched earth.
And so I forget, and the day becomes a smoldering inkwell
Splashed by the stiffened limbs of evening

Across the slats of whitewashed fences,
And I forget the traces of your devotions wept
Into the mad chalice of moments without end,
And I forget your cheekbones that float in the dark,

And the smell of your muffled voice
Thrown off like a wet cloak in the wind,
And the waves of creatures crunching over you
In the starry pasture,

I forget the flames of this invisible life
That sometimes make small flashes across your urban hillside,
I forget and walk off into the dying world without you
And the memory of your laughter that keeps clawing at the void.

Some Days Are Like This, While Others Aren't

I caught myself perverting all the laws
Of taxidermy in a dream state,
So I went ahead and made an offering,
The spindly helix of some translucent fever

Squirming across the net of my own rising heat,
Its purpose known to myself and it alone.
I felt intent on keeping it this way, and when ready,
To cool myself down into a tame and weighted thing,

And suck the being (if one can call it that)
Back through the night's dilations
With the elephantine stealth of an unrecorded tribe.
I think I may have in fact accomplished something

In the throes of all this drama, something no doubt emptied
Of the held breath of an underwater soul,
And the closed-eyed dizziness
Of its whole stuffed zoo of wavy icons,

But really, I cannot yet see what it can be,
As I seem to have overshot my heartbeat once again,
And the free-floating boomerang of my yearning dictates

That my head remain bowed in this eternal act
Of deference or exhaustion.

The Poem of Force

AFTER SIMONE WEIL'S ESSAY ON *The Iliad*

How often have I lain beneath a roof of trees and sestinas,
Sestinas and trees, the chiasmus of my timid hopes decked
Out in the styles of the day,
Losing myself in novels of corporeal sunshine and a home
Where a samovar is always gurgling on the stove, and men of frivolous
    or serious wives
Tie self-strung misery around their necks. And knowledge

Is a shining lamp that lights the hieroglyphs of love and suffering, and no knowledge
Is enough to put it out. I used to dream of a sestina
Whose very presence would ignite the longing of an ancient wife
Who'd swim the matrices of grace into the waves that swept the deck
Of a ship leaving its home
Of drowsy cows and frogs waiting by the river as the day

Blinked over never-ending fields. But today
I feel in almost perfect balance with the world, and any knowledge
That I had or have is but a lying down in the glass casket of my thoughts, the long
    small home
I can barely even find were it not for this sestina
Crashing like painted rain against my eyes decked
With brazen orchid light. And were I not a wife

And mother to these thoughts, I'd take my wifely
Ringless hand and draw the curtains on the days
Of an atavistic reaching out and clear the deck
For something more untoward than the acknowledgment
That we are riveted between laughter and the abyss, like characters in a sestina
With all the lines crossed out. I find my home

When I travel the near and distant byways, I find my home

With the wives

Of absent heroes put to sleep in the sleep of bronze, and in sestinas

That haven't borne witness to a single day

Of war, arrows flying on both sides but none to pierce the knowledge

That we ourselves are a deck

Of marked cards that decorate

The history of our homeless

Tribe. To know

This is to understand Hector's grief for the long-robed wives

As he stood outside Troy's walls in the rising of the day

Waiting for his death, and trembling, his soul mourning its fate of being
    trapped inside a thing—to understand this is to return to an age of
    epics, not sestinas.

For now I have only the bare knowledge of all wives

Who've ever decked their homes

With the talismans of the day, and my talismans are sestinas.

Entry

The luckless perambulator whistling down this street
The mollycoddled volcano X-ing out its mysteries
The oh boy of stations leaving me behind

I ask myself, what is this life?

What is this life with its risen characters
What is this life with its new cartoons
What is this tonality that lags

Brave animal of eternal valor
Isn't it enough that I exist?

Emergency Kisses, Tectonic Smiles

With large dark eyeballs
The caitiffs of the moon drink their ratty hemlock.
In a garden of delight, I swear by the setting of a tortoise.
And those who swim swimmingly along,
Tracing leaves, peeling a zero,
They offer me emergency kisses, tectonic smiles,
A baptism in an asylum of geese.
Wound of day on my thigh, hydraulic reason,
I wrap myself in the firmness of mountains,
Reach out toward a flaccid idol
Carousing through a trumpet blast.
It is written that we breathe out our measures
Through a wax paper blizzard.
And, we have fashioned ourselves out of moist germs.
I've heard it said that regardless of the cost,
If you breathe more than your own breath,
Your fair share of nowhere will certainly be lost.

The sum of suns burns itself in effigy.
Monster, you've created me.

Home of the Cubit Idea

"Your dizzy is my dizzy," she said,
And, "I'll give you a swift kick in your apocrypha."
Then there was the smudge of elements
On an empty Sunday, a long bird flying overhead.
Freedom came gusting in, the yonder of his reflections.
"I covenant you, my paramour, my satellite.
You are all potential, the coin before it's been called,
The future without a gloaming.
You eat in my house and in a full saloon-
Girl suit, you salute me. Giddyup!"
They lived in an arena of tangents,
Yet the tangential was as close to them as a stigmatic sun
Waking on bloodied snowcaps.
Let's just say they had syntax on their hands,
And torched their burnished grammar to the hilt.
Things sat around in pots for weeks and sprouted.
Then *they* sprouted, and kept sprouting,
And still, kept sprouting.
Finally, they moved far away from the small violence
Of their younger days to a star-shaped apartment in a field.
They missed their old crazy vegetation
But found that telling a good joke over a stale beer
Is just as satisfying and, in fact, emotionally healthier.
But their corn still goes, "Rye!"
The potted plant goes, "La, la."

Fortune Seals Itself Around My Breathing and All I'm Known by Dwindles

Show me your green world,
Animal in estrus.
The planar energy that exists
Without shading, without undressing,
This is your calling
That wears its olive center
In a shameless dance of lariats and leis.
Everything is wrong,
The wursts have legs,
I sleep on a deathbed of arms,
I suffer a loss so anemic
My mind swims like an alarm.
Youth is not a storehouse
For *Here, go fetch this*
And *How big is your teapot?*
There are javelins in my rose
Garden, suitcases on the waves,
And I wear a histological
Shawl (citrus flavored)
To my pinwheel seizure
Where Uncle Buster
Stumbles, 81, drunk and naked,
And tells me, *Watch out,*
The sadness has bones in it.
He could light the ozone
On fire, poor horseman,
And for this reason,
And for this reason alone,
I bow down in the mustached
Alleys with my childless shame.

The Puppet's Dream

An alliance smothers wholly
While green gumdrops take shape
Out of sheer fear of being alone.

To wrest love out of a sleeping body
Is like counting the deer in the fields in the evening.

"She's not a friend, just someone
Who won't let go."

We needed more plastic, more metal,
So you went down and collected it,
You went out and forested it.
You were frail like an electric moon.

Then the world got small and ugly.
Stoned, you noticed the dragon is everything.
Then said something trite and stupid.
Then, the mellifluous agony of the puppet's dream,

A savage listening.

Neptune

I saw my love shoot up the intravenous moonlight,
Vanished in a Milky Way of negatives.
I saw Neptune's navel in a garden of starfish
And swore I'd never step there.
I saw my car with its little blue belly
Ride through an auditorium of anthems
That will never sound the same.
I repented the fragrance of a garland of limes
Reflected in a monastic swimming pool.
The power lines went gray and Sunday
So I jangled my construction paper prayers
Over bedside promises of epiphany and bread.
Guardian of my own knucklebone,
I hit an inkblot and the inkblot hit a tree
And became limp as the word grief.
To weep the trills that do not dearly
Means improvement is merely improvement
And it is arbitrary that we age.
But if I stepped on Neptune, I would find
A vatic searing library announcing your arrival
And I would stand far back in a garden of starfish
Growing legs for each one severed.

St. Mark's Planetarium

I was a star and it was boring.
Informed of my quadratics,
At home with my hang-ups and trips,
There were totems, tolls and ribbons,
Deathly paintings of stairs.
It was a reincarnation I have never felt,
Yanking brute ions in streams of the reciprocal.
I lay my hands on the ore of my failures
And remained on a hillside, covered in claws.
It was still early, the recycling hadn't come.
Mediocre ran up my throat
Like a lawn in heat. I loved it.
I loved it so much there was a ceremony:
Nests in flames, the nests of palace spiders.

Trio

Persephone would lie awake nights,
Beating off, thinking about Olive.
Olive had eyes only for Roger
Who didn't give her a second thought.
Roger waited on a precipice every first
Day of spring for Persephone
To appear with her long flaming hair
Parted by the sun's sleek rays.
He'd say, "Snatch what's in the sky,
It might be venison, dear deer."
Persephone would answer, "My
Days are longer now, and still I pine
For my beloved Olive." Olive joined
Them both for dinner at the Macaroni Grill,
Munching on peppercorns and washing them
Down with copious amounts of white wine.
"When you're dealing with mental illness,
You're dealing with money," she'd say,
And the rhinestone castle of her dreams
Where she'd be tucked away with Roger
Materialized on the polished wood
Floor as her lithium level dropped and dropped.
Roger sighed. Persephone sighed while
Olive drunkenly envisioned a blue house,
The fragile still life of vernal stars
Above it that Persephone would paint
Later that night in Roger's Orphic sleep.

In the Barn, with Crayons

We drank wine from the galaxy,
Mixed blasphemy with sangria,
We were sentinels of Being,
I added my force to yours.

There were love songs in the bathwater,
There was also the rhetoric of a photograph
Torn in two.

Then we were a bored mitosis,
Lugubriously meditating on the forever of it.
We knew better, we knew different, we knew nothing.
I was a vase of dried commas.

Then the stars cast our light,
We knew nothing of photographs, of wine, of Being.
Devout, I sang, "Your mittens are making me nervous"
While you froze in the arctic cold.

We need a good ending to this.
We need no ending at all.
What we need is a bad fluency in the night,
To keep the exile from coming.

You Know, Half-Night?

Syringes linked together like bloody angels,

I see it, I report it, I am the last leaf

Designated to cling to a tree in winter.

And then you came back, colorless.

You rose from your slab One More Time,

An animal with no chance at the dawn's migration.

Call it an arrowhead, call it a dart, it's all the same.

You were an energy that waltzed above me

Like a dancing flea, when everything sings

After a hurricane in the quivering damp.

You watched the wind with dumbfounded grace,

Sank your teeth into the neck of death,

Followed its bits of flesh into the darkness.

Factory Days

An Aristotelian impulse, linearly placed,
Garbled up the machinery we used
To make eggs. Two eggs, four eggs, eight
Million eggs, and then suddenly no eggs

At all. And the love we had for each other,
That was gone, too, but this wasn't as bad
As the absence of eggs. So instead of eggs,
We began to make absinthe and at first

The love grew even more than when we
Had the eggs but then, well, you can imagine
The rest. This is about when I thought
I could go for a fantastic pedicure and I did

Exactly that and found this was the precise
Happiness I'd hoped for during all my years
Of making eggs. When it was over,
A long line of land fauna crossed my path,

Unlike any I had ever seen before or since.
I mean, have you ever had your style cramped
By a wicker basket, had your mind pierced
With red hoop earrings, knowing what would come

Next would be a trough of lamentations? I haven't,
But the fauna knew it well. Turns out some
Of them made eggs, too, and the love that each
One had for the other was purely platonic.

How ironic, I reflected, then traveled back
To the absinthe factory humming *The Star-
Spangled Banner* on my first birthday without eggs,
The shining sea warbling above us all.

The Mall Hookers

Hi!

I'm back, singing, the core of the earth is a giant,
Singing, the core of the earth is a saw-toothed plant.

I walked promptly to my Dumbaholics
Anonymous meeting and shared about my fear
Of the mall hookers that come disguised with babies.
I sold all my land back to the fiery archipelago,
Bought a plot of rubber trees in the generous afternoon,
And then it hit me, my camouflage is unworthy
To hide my outcast spirit glimmering
In a crowded restaurant on this hot day in June.

Hell, what do I, who weeps prairies
Every night from a hopscotch box,
What do I know about the mall
Hookers, lamp-lit canoes haunting fickle rivers
In flowery skirts and breasts swollen with blue milk?
I decided they're really bank robbers with perfumed notes
That read, *I have a booby trap, give me all your money.*
Yeah, that must be it, and finally I could sing again,

The core of the earth is a giant,
The core of the earth is a saw-toothed plant.

Positive Monsters

Someone can just pull you out
Of your car at any moment, I thought,
That day a very fat man stole my clothes
From the laundromat. I am piratical,
Filching limes from the positive monsters
That drink suds from the machines,
The bottom of my world dropping out
All the time. But the suds are a dowry,
The insane sediment of this place
I inhabit, this nausea hockey I know,
Blending a hiss with a science.
I require one Diesel per hour,
A mixed drink of eagles and ice,
While stoned poets burn themselves up
In teleporters just to get to NY for a night.

2.

The jeany blue sleeplessness of knees
Of an oversexed voice major
Is what I would add to the phrase,
They are no longer a sexual unit.
I bought a wedding present for a couple
I didn't like. It was a tea set and two limes.
I said, *Many years of happiness* while dinner
Was served in brief, clouded wisps.
I was subconsciously planning my own downfall,
A decent flowering zooming skyward, then falling,
Falling, "desiring to leave this place forever."
The guard dog that doubles as a therapy dog
Barked fiercely in my direction
As if to remind me that this place I inhabit,
I think it's very good.

Why Not Cleveland?

Wake up in a thaumaturgic churchyard, O!

Unshatterable kernel of night at heart of day, O!

And the child cries out because he has no mother,

The child cries out because she has no brother,

This story is as full of holes as a trepanist's head.

I could get a good job flipping biscuits anywhere,

But it wouldn't be the same, the gunmetal

Witching hour spreading over the sky like a birthday cake,

Your concussion on the wooden flowers,

The ultraviolet of our parallel paths,

Dawnlessness.

For Damon

I suck at foosball but that's okay.

I'm really simple but that's okay.

And you, all blue stomach and sky,

Morning eaten dry by limber alphabets,

Bless the fire, bless the devil's rain.

I have given up the greenness of my spirit

With yours, my toasted animal, my breath.

Without

These are the desolate dark streets

Where sparrows fall and die

Before 4 o'clock crashing

Into parkas into loneliness into the unfathomability

Of crosses hung on dogwood centuries

These are winter these are spring

These are the limbic notions

Aftertaste warm in cyanide

Glasses riddled with lips with eyes with present

Jeeps shoes acrostic fevers

Breaking speed of ash ten eleven twelve thirteen

And no one, no one came

This

Your piece I entitled "This"
Is on now, and I am clumsy
With CDs, as if I enter a field
Of antelopes, swaying drunk, ripping
Through like a silk dress in a Laundromat
Dryer. The unthought remains unsaid,
And now I can unleash
You, unleash my need to be need,
And I say this with fear and trembling.
There was never any real cruelty
Between us in the sunsets
Dripping down in bloody pools,
Our words crashing more like waves
That flatten into surf, not meant to destroy
But to say, *There is too much world.*
If I have ever pretended
To plant more than my share of beans
Beneath the beanstalks that rise like palaces,
I will consider myself unworthy to visit your tree,
In all of its leafy destiny.
You'd often say that we were siblings.
I section off an orange,
In the end, the color of our love.

After His Woman Is Killed, Conan the Barbarian Goes On to Become a King by His Own Hand, with Her Spirit Guiding Him

Beautiful lipids

The madness of negatives

Last night the tall dead

Walked the village like giants

While I shot up in a dream

Shall I make sense or shall

I tell the truth—choose either

I cannot do both.

Kind eyes, an unmade bed,

I know you are reading this

As I go. I go, not quite as doctrinaire

As an atheist, I will bend

Someday like a reed over the broken

Mosaic of a suburb, my home you,

Your home, me, and those who

Understand will also die.

"You are the most alive thing in the world"

You too, in my world and in the other one.

Amen.

No Poem

Death encamps the lucky.

Life encamps the ____.

Drizzle of tennis shoes

Upon a shrill tenement

Want, my name is legion

I pick and cut across

Nature's axles

Don't make me your teacher

Fringes of daylight sight the numbers

Of women getting dressed

To the soft, alluvial motions

Under the heart-attack orange sky

This un-God

Night

I Am the Arm

Mortal cornflakes in an agey oven.

Pivot the small blisters.

Chain love oft betokens *so near*

Braids into humid the L escaping

Sea urchin with lemon—appreciate finality

-ied -ied -ied

Bleeds into stasis

Bleeds into stasis

Or merely bleeds

Death Sonnet

Electrolyte my vivid exile,
Swallow fizzy tongues,
Violet 6 and violent triage
When all has come undone.

Electrolyte me baby—
Exile from your tongue,
Violent triage, there you go
We're vividly undone.

Toothsome lathe and lithesome tooth,
Syphilis on a rack,
Exile all the fizzies,
You're never coming back.

You're never coming back, my love,
You're never coming back.

"You Will *Always* Be My Animal"

I fathom your blue-green essence

Against the corrosive red fibers of the day.

In reaching toward you my arms catch fire.

In attempting to touch you they blossom into ash.

They mingle with yours forever and forever and forever.

Too often, you are only a shadow cast

Across an endless sunny Wednesday:

Trapezoidal sleep, spell-check aflame with saints,

Roseate silo, the arrows are dark, the moment sharp.

This Is What You Get

I want to be intimate with everyone,

And most of all with you, my only.

I want to taste the flavor of a leaf

On a stained glass house,

Wear the collar of a pregnant deli cat

In all of her betokened squalor.

Is it the full blossom of the evening,

Or the full flower of the evening

That drags its wings across our crumbled street

As I listen to your voice, getting younger

Now, as I wait, miles ahead of and miles behind

My time, a train that hovers here suspended

Over a warm pool of numbers, never adding up

Or subtracting delicately away.

Hirsute Blossoms Crashed into the Season, Exoskeletons of Zeros Netted the Wind

The answers are stuck like tiny eggs
Between my teeth, a cosmic arithmetic

Wending its way through depilation
And the subtle centrifuge of forgotten

Territories, which I oil and burn,
Crazy with black festivals

Against a knotted skyline, pop-
Up ads for growing taller,

A concupiscent halo that invites
Wire, wire, wire, wire, wire,

Until we meet again in the crossing
Of the bridge between the I

And the you, which would open out before us,
If only I could creep into the vespers

Of the lucid Law you know,
Sun setting over the burning territories,

Incinerating me every night
Into the dawn's charred aviary, the word.

12th Wedding Anniversary

Jailed and decreased, my doughnuts rise.

Have a feather, don't ask why,

There is a Coney Island in my eye.

Hair and plaid rabbits,

Anniversal belief is the strongest to go

Over a listless sky, a prevenient frost.

Let's go to the Cloisters

And all-you-can-eat sushi,

My tattoo should be healed now.

Dear, you are a norming legend in the kitty-star.

I eat for two, on the evening of

We knew each other before our faces and our names.

12/24/04
_____

Anchored to a wood floor,

Cheating the avenues, I potato

You, I potato you. Riding the eve

Of good gumdrops, the folds of

A calla lily spin to Muzak,

Sciatica-pink and missing a microchip.

It was easy for us in that time.

There we stood, grossed out by a sage's

Tongue wagging around a lightbulb.

To say I miss you, is to say that the sky

Is a paper cliff I leap from

In order to avoid the affluence of the starlight.

And yet I miss you. A three-foot-tall

Orange cat leaps from my dream onto

A fire hydrant and I set sail upon the seven seas,

Looking for you in every pair of eyes

And finding you, yes, in every pair of eyes.

Once Upon a Time in America

Here in this room I slept in
As you lay dead and alone
After you died, while I, superstitious
Peasant, slept, slept through
Phone call after phone call from
Detective after detective, finally
Waking to Daniel's simple and beatific
Damon's dead, and me waking up
Lizzette, breaking the news,
Making arrangements like a cop
Or fireman, taking a few minutes
To say I love you to the morning sky,
I still have never let anyone see me cry.
Never having been one of the fully
Living, I live, half of me in
A cornfield filled with skyscrapers,
Half of me in that place we are
Before we're born and after we die.
Tonight I was outside thinking
Of that holy drunken terror
Jackson Pollock. *Fuck you moon*,
He'd shout and cry. A big dog
Came running up to me and his owner
Shouted, *Jackson, come back here.*
You my teacher, died unknown
And there's nothing for me to do
About it right now except to write
Your legacy no matter how inept
I can be. My phone rings.
I slide across pink ice to get it.
The splotched cat returns home.
When I asked you for a sign,
The fireplace doors shattered.

You are a dead musician who died
Alone. I wait to go to you,
Smoking and breaking curses under
The Jackson Pollock fuck you moon.

If You Can? What Do You Mean, If You Can?

The daisies are running under an umbrella
Of French fries.
Into the mud, through the bush,
X sails screaming on a plate of asthma.
Discourse thickens the soup.
I am a paycheck.
I've washed away my sins,
Even the ones the campfire blessed.
I can't breathe.
Or: I can blow so hard out of my blowhole
I eat my fingertips like popcorn.
I'm dishonest yet aboveboard.
I'm a wacko. Om.
I can dish it out and yet.
I'm a widow. I'm fatherless.
Pliant anesthetic, hail to you.

Against Brilliance

The waters are very simple today.

Hospital blue, in error of twilight,

The sound of one hand clapping in a star-shaped womb.

Having never felt twice about the same flecked river,

You can either swim or hide your eyes away.

I piss in it and eat all the fish raw.

Poem for Paul Vee

Mercury in perpetual retrograde,
It doesn't matter. A tether of
Highbrow verbals distemper
The flies. Across gender bromides,
Across anthems, say cheese.
I wear a habit in my mind,
And that's OK. I am a neediness
And a Rule. To think some remedial
Goose would hammer anticlimactic
Spring, summer, fall, now winter;
It's crazy what you find converging
In the underworld. Surrender.
And you: a desert plant sprouting
Futures over the open-hearted earth.

A Day without a Date

The foggy entrances, the stone-
Cold awakenings, the sea is shiny
And green. We had a contract
In the other world, shiny green
And blue, now it's solitaire
And another memory and another.
What a child you were, with a fondness
For the truth, the sunflowers,
The daisies, the skein of yarn
At the cat's feet, the background
Pulling at you, red and black.
Now I wander around like a derelict
In a dirty parka, you you you
Around my neck, on my finger,
Inside me, always inside me.
To say I love you is to say
That the wind loves the rock
And the sea reveals itself timelessly,
And that I am very very tired
But not asleep, love, I am not asleep.

Tribute #2

I predict that instead of one
I will be two.
I predict that if ever I was
To fuck anyone, we would be three.
I predict that if ever we were to have
A child, there would be four.
I predict that I will never fuck
Anyone ever again.
I predict I will have at least
Five more cats this lifetime.
I predict long gyrations of thought
In the grass.
I predict a wild wind in academia.
I predict I will wave a broken wand
Across the universe.
I predict that you are a river and a tree.
I predict nothing.
I predict the end of my predictions,
And the loss of the whole world
At your brilliant shadow,
And that I will continue to hum
Your buried music like a refrigerator
Deep into the night.

The poem is elusive.
And so are you.
Hair dripping with laxatives,
Laundry on fire,
It is better to wait than to carry.
Brush your face lest it falls off.
Eat your sleeves. There.
Love is.
Hither I suffer. Thither I suffer. Hither I suffer.
And if you come across a tiny thing,
Don't believe it.
Tomorrow is a bar of soap
In the twinkle twinkle.
And pain. And laundry. And pain.

Raving Urn

FOR KAT

I wanted to write you
The most beautiful poem

In the world. Straining
Through gray screens,

Stammering Italian verbs,
A capsized wok is filled

With snow peas, opulent
Scat in the background,

As nails of rain pin night's
Tapestry to our un-

Curtained window.
Getting up in the morning

Is foreign to me. I still don't
Know how to put a sheet

On the bed. An empty urn
Raves in a closet. My diet

Is shit. If it's truth you want,
Walk slowly down the street,

Shop for exotic pets,

Emulate skin-fire in a laughing

Gold box and wait for dusk
On an anonymous tightrope.

Everything good'll come your way.

I Am Impatient

I am impatient to be well again,
As the spring's false hope
Skates idly on the surface of last winter.
I am impatient to sleep the sleep of the dreamless
And wake to a line of coffee grounds
On the dirty surface of our sink.
I am impatient to step lightly
From word onto thing,
To meet my mind's umbrella
Grazing on a wet field.
The world is no longer the same,
But I am no longer the same.
I carry you with me like a song
In my head, a kaleidoscope of colors
Parading across a landscape in which a scene
Of seduction unfolds on a rakishly tilted
Group of rocks or on a closed space
Covered by a canopy of leaves.
Do you remember how all the shadows
Were right for the season, our season,
And how everything was both
As encyclopedic and clear as the
Complex data of vision fashioned out of error
And the ravages of time?
We shook like petals on boiling water.
I am impatient to break like a meteor
Upon your sealed world, impatient
To decipher those cryptographic symbols
Drifting through the shadowless ambience
That time and time presents itself:
The pink slow blossoming of a summer night
Tied like a tourniquet around your arm

That, sleeved in a newly ironed shirt,
Both draws me and prevents me
From drawing close to you.

Nature Poem

Behind a pasture, swaying,
A skyline of fickle pines.
Like-minded sweeping
Scraps the warmth of gestures.
Too late, I say, too late,
For us to cuddle the canary's
Stubbled song.
There is a lifeline waiting.
No one is coming.
The study of heat blinks
In the midday sun.
Soon, a blaze of rhyme
Will cast an artificial glare
And sunset on the windowsill.
Good for us, who die in flames.
Good for us who walk among the ghosts.

Damage Control

Quiet, I am a machine
With emotions.
Exposed, I forget who I am.
Cider eyes have sunk
Like punctured rocks.
Did you ever unfurl
Yourself beyond the scribbles
And whisper to the shore?
We are sentinels with
Our ears torn off.
You cannot ghost me
Into pixels. I'm on
My own here, I guess,
Like all the times before
The starry threshold
Of two alarms sounding
Became one. Only one,
But one.

Newborn

The dead
Ruffle my feathers
With their thundering no's.
History = sycamore
Turning in the dark green fire.
I've eaten the delicious grass.
I cry even then.
I also laugh and laugh again.

5/30/06

Every day can't be Christmas,
Mon cher. We are tires.
Without spokes, so silver
When the day is silver, too.
Every day we walk
With trees sprouting out of engines,
We wait for some clear answer
Funneled through our sacred
Wants. We want. We can't.
But who is to say that candy
Will not fall through our hands,
Take what we've spoken
In hushed voices, streaming silver
In the blighted day. I never knew
You. Or, I knew what is loved
So dearly, a knitted sweater
Wet and hanging from some
Mangled hanger, without any
Chance for burn. You told me
Once that our lives were stolen.
I know now that our lives were free.

Autobiography

I chose the path of sorrow in the green green wood.
Not the ochre flakes raining down
Upon the raining down,
Not the harvest moon,
The corpulent pet,
The ambitious first name I own without socks,
Not the lost numbers, the copper bosom
Of a wavy moth without blank pages—
None of these things will allay my velvety hangover.
The meat is of the halcyon variety.
The last time I inherited a factory, I slid my lip
Into a skeptic's pointed question,
And poured out honey onto those who protest ants.
But I chose the path of sorrow in the green green wood,
And this was the final time a mother's answers
Filled a white basin with those who suffer and are pleased.

One Poem for Matthew Z.

Whatever what is, is, has to align.
Dreamers we with our hands
In the honey, fret not the insurrection
Of the senses when a cold star ceases.
The undertow is blank and stays
In mourning. Shadow-boxing
Tatterdemalion, oh, there are only
So many words. Let be. Truth
And sorrow are brothers, no?
The cat is whining for affection,
The way I was whining for affection
For awhile. The second time
I'd ever heard my name spoken
With such care, a bum had just
Put a cross on my husband's grave
And showed it to me. What does
All of this mean, Matthew? Am I
To assume the reality lies within
A mosquito trapped in amber?
That the French have no word for mother?

Star of the Sea

I put the fear of God into a radish,
And ate it whole—*moing!*

Really, no taste of lamb chops
Kept me quiet,

As the night's spokes fought
Wild over tepid ice.

I slept through the rapture,
O! And returned to find

A stifling load. I fixed it,
Once, I fixed it twice,

I doubted a hand over
Too many stones.

Love, my wintering toy
To watch its leavesongs

On my silly gong.
I guess that's why it's called

The fruit of blanks,
Always succor,

Never ill-conceived.

Elko the Desert Dog

Elko stayed home from
The robot parade,
The invitation aflame
Like a paper crane,

The pointy-faced one
With a leaf for a friend
Ate nothing but flies
For a week without end.

Elko says, "Don't rhyme,
Don't rhyme,
When you do my stomach
Churns with chyme,"

So I will pay homage,
Put an end to this mess,
And honor the big E
In a sun-tattered dress:

The one and only Elko
Who came down from space
Is like a brief wisp
In a giant place.

Zero

A dog barks in
The theoretical cold.
We shake our fists at him,
Wandering beneath the furze.
The antisocial wends.
Too much life is a banana
In the angling daylight.
Don't superlative me, friend.
I've already washed my placard
Of a sun rising in no particular direction,
And given it to the last
Who will be first
And the first who will be last.

Soporific Jungles

These are the days where fire
Stings the eyes. Meat gets
Crisp, the giraffe rings out.
Too fast the lemming bands
Marching two by two into blonde.
A lone palm tree sparkles with the wonderment
Of a girl, obvious and bright in the heraldic air.
No one cares, in this real jungle of buildings,
Stickball bat splinters and handball halves.
A cigarette is all she needs
To plug the dream-mares in.

Dirge

Too late a small vigil
Running softly into

Rainwater, too late
A history ascertained.

Here there is peace
Without a small fire,

A small crisis washed
In lostness.

We waited in the rain
While the people

Went off somewhere.
Too late a small

Vigil running softly,
Too late a history

On a pyre without
Our gentle reasons.

The people went off
Somewhere, too late

A history ascertained,
A small vigil washed

Us of our gentle reasons,
Our lostness a small pyre

Washed in crises
Without reason.

We sang something
And all was washed in rain

Singing to us
Of our lostness

As we stood vigil
To our history ascertained.

If the Earth Is a School

There is the part
That connects you to all creation.
Then there is the part
That tells you,
You must go to the store for cigarettes,
Or your students all look totally deformed.
Which part is you?
My cigarette burns a hole
In the night sky,
My students are soul-animals
Without a shepherd.
I don't know which way is the right way,
Nor do I understand physics.
What I understand is "I'm hungry"
And "I need to sleep,"
And all poets and poetry elude me,
Especially myself and my own.

A Wish That All Could Remain the Same

Toy insects populate latitudes.
There is a blue sun yonder.
The sky is playful and green.
Who am I writing this for,
In the green, ever-changing chain
Of adverbs? Heavy-handed
Strings of music whip me,
Hold me close. Vienna is far away,

But you are close, closer than
What I'm able to fathom in my pain.
There is a love that remains,
Is all that remains, after dying.
This is what I mean when I say
Hold me, as black insomnia breeds.

Love's Only Seed

Mercury on a corpulent
Sunbather, armpits protest.
See, in a poem, things actually
Have to be doing things,
Not just floating around.
The china closet is all messed
Up. You won't find any drugs.
Listen, I said it before, die
And come back as fire. Listen.
I said it: fire. Were you listening?
If you were, can you get me a tea?

On the Death of My Mother's Cat

I'd like to write a good poem,
An honest poem. A poem without
Melodrama or death in it. But it
Seems that everything has death
In it these days, and for that I am
Truly sad. I'd like to write a poem
About my father, but I never knew
My father. I'd like to write a poem
About a tree house, but I was never
In a tree house. But this empty bowl,
What is my relationship to it? That
I wonder, more so than what makes
This tidy watered-downness cover
Us. The imitative fallacy is oh so—
I wonder what the chaos of the sun was
To her eyes before they closed.

The Peace That So Lovingly Descends

"You" have transformed into "my loss."
The nettles in your vanished hair
Restore the absolute truth
Of warring animals without a haven.
I know, I'm as pathetic as a railroad
Without tracks. In June, I eat
The lonesome berries from the branches.
What can I say, except the forecast
Never changes. I sleep without you,
And the letters that you sent
Are now faded into failed lessons
Of an animal that's found a home. This.

Acknowledgments

I would like to thank Charlie Wright for his profound vision and generosity, Joshua Beckman for his genius in making beautiful books and for being loving to me when things were dire, Matthew Zapruder, Anthony McCann, and Matthew Rohrer for their wise artistic guidance and friendship, my parents, Jo-Ann and Jack Sleight, Peter Bartók, Paul Vlachos, Lizzette Potthoff, Monica Antolik, Adam Skalman, Peggy Munson, Gordon Ramsey, Curtis McCartney, Daniel Kramoris, Walter P. Knake, Jr., Euclid, Obi, Elko, and all the other angels in my life, both human and divine, and I would like to thank Damon Tomblin, my soulmate, husband, and artistic mentor, who was so good as to share himself completely with me throughout the course of our union and without whose presence none of these poems could have been written. Finally, I would like to thank the Father and the Son, for giving me everything I have ever needed throughout my lifetime, and for infinitely blessing my path.